Life in Pieces

Casey Tarr

Presentation by *BookLeaf Publishing*

Web: www.bookleafpub.com

E-mail: info@bookleafpub.com

ISBN: 9789357440691

First edition 2023

To my boys, the hairs may be grayer and the house may be louder..but I wouldn't trade a second of being your mom for the world.

And to the infamous Grammie Norma - for showing us that life is always worth living.

ACKNOWLEDGEMENT

I never thought I'd get this far, so bear with me as I write this out (memory isn't my strongest aspect).

Kurt, thanks for always putting up with my crazy ideas. I'd be lost in this life without you at my side.

Jamie - my built in best friend who welcomed me at day one of my life as the best big sister ever. For challenging me at my reading, and encouraging my writing. For being there unconditionally during all the moments that have happened, and will happen. You rock.

My parents, who taught me to work hard and to always make good choices. Here's hoping this book is a testament to both.

And to every single friend, teacher, patient, and family member along my life path that has helped create moments in my life. It's because of you that I could write all of this.

Newborn

Ten fingers,
Ten toes,
Love beyond what my heart knows.

Two eyes,
Two ears,
Completely captivate me with fear.

Breathe in,
Breathe out,
Exuding renewal without doubt.

Softness,
Grace,
Brilliant motion in place.

Peaceful heart,
Innocent mind,
Embraces by love and consumed by pride.

Toddler

2

Run,
Don't walk.
Scream,
Don't talk.

Happy,
Scars,
Living life
Without a care.

Can't sleep,
Too tired.
Read me
One more story.

Love,
Fight,
Day and night.
Please be there for me.

Teenager

Young
Silly and Stylish
Or so I think
And you
Old

Brave
Resilient and loud
Finding my place in the world
Words can hurt
Fearful

Wonder
Full of knowledge
Smarter than parents are
Full of doubt
Uncertainty

Will
Spite and sass
The world won't see me coming.
Go forth
Succeed

College Years

The directions
Life can go,
When you trek out
On your own.

Terrified to face it.
Prepared to leave.
Knowing nothing.
Your life, ready to seize.

Knowledge is power.
Experience is pain.
With each step,
Everything to gain.

New love, new life,
Independence grows bold.
All cards on the table,
Bracing from a fold.

Backwards or center,
Right or left.
Growth will await you,
With each passing breath.

Heartbreak / Goodbye

It burns
The coffee on my lap
It burns
But it will never be that bad

That bad
Is the way he left my sight
That bad
Is the way it ended that night

That night
When reality was blurred
That night
When I wasn't seen or heard

The noise
He said words that broke my heart
That noise
Fear, anger, emotions broke apart

It burns
Knowing nothing last forever
It burns
Knowing some ties must be severed.

Forever

Denial of love
Friendship too valued to share
Divided by feelings
Too bold to share

Forbidden, it felt
On high alert, yet restless
Wanting with uncertainty
Until rendered breathless

Protection I knew
Faithful beyond any doubt
Necessary steadiness
Strength life can't be without

Joining together
Two lives become united
Linked through grace and understanding
To never be divided

Motherhood

Tears came the day the two lines shown
Revealing an unknown fate
My heart confused as it could be
Unsure if joy or fear it should take

Prepared, deserving
How could I be?
Just a child at heart
Yet, you were given to me

A young bride with life ever changing
Wondering, waiting
A strong, youthful body
Evolving and creating

And then, like a storm
Apprehension set in
Would I be everything
Worth your heart in the end

You came, I breathed
Without doubt in that moment
My heart prepared to take
All your life's opponents

I held your hand
You held my heart
Bound by blood
Never apart

Creating Identity

Degrees,
Hard knocks
Building a profession.

Passion,
Driven,
Working and living.

Tired,
But needed.
Focus all over.

Who you are,
What you do.
Finding joy in becoming.

1st Steps

Up.
Up, down, up.
Cry.
Try, cry, try.

How?
Knee bends.
Fall.
Try, cry, try.

Stand.
One foot, two.
Walk.
Try and try.

Smile.
Step, step, step.
Run.
Laugh, go, live.

Love Again

You were you
From the start
No expectations
Love flowing from our hearts

Sweet innocence
Given a family name
Knowing you will
Create your own claim to fame

Fiercely independent
Smiles filled with joy
Infectious bursts of laughter
Our sweet little boy.

Completing our small family,
Making sure your presence be known.
The world forever thankful
For the shine for all your glow.

Strength

Rains pour
Anger flows like thunder rolls
Stronger, closer
Daunting

Words said
Frustration flies like blackbirds
Heavy, harsh
Unequivocal

Inside, fortitude
Fighting with potency of a soldier
Resilient, tenacious
Progressive

A weathered storm
Strength as the fruitful winner
Witnessed, forgiven
Persevered

Nature

We breathe in the air
And block out reality
We step towards the sun
And change our mentality

Feet to the dirt
Skin to the waves
Eyes to the heavens
Thankful for days

Embracing the solitude
Thankful for all she shows
Mother Nature guides
We follow where she goes

Rivers bring us curiosity
Lakes bring us joy
Mountain roads, they lead us
A brilliant and welcomed decoy

In the great outdoors
We set in our roots
Settling in for the sunset
With our broke in old boots.

Believe

Excitement building
Belief in every breath.
Waiting, wondering,
Anticipating.

Could it be?
What do I hear?
Puffs of air.
Steps.

Peeking around corners,
Open the door.
Milk, cookies,
Gone.

Sprint back to bed,
Is morning here?
Eyes closed,
Asleep.

Morning air,
Charged with life.
Joy, faith,
Believe.

90

County roots
Country heart
Streaks of reddish hair
Full of spark

Sincere sister
Mother of four
Guardian of
The revolving door

Lover of fun
Believer in hard work
Fearless leader
And friend to the dirt

Destroyer of hunger
Provider of love
Creator of magic
And all things thereof

Years of true perseverance
Days loved in the sun
Celebration of vibrancy
At 90 years young.

Be Brave

Mountains are high
With peaks touching the sky
Don't let it intimidate you.

Doors to the unknown
Prevent light from being shown.
Don't stop believing that it's there.

First steps are hard.
Ten miles feels like one yard.
Don't let it keep you from running.

Bravery in your feet
No challenge you can't defeat.
Find pride in what you are.

Pandemic

Start
To be normal
Free to decide
Rise

Begin
To question
Fear bubbling inside
Prepare

Panic
Feeding the fire
New leaders emerge
Control

Steady
Attempting comprehension
Finding a need
Unsettling

Bravery
Eyes skyward
Opening the gates
Unity

Farm Life

Up at dawn,
A crop to tend.
Prayers for rain,
Then sun again.

Youthful spirits
And old alike,
Push forward the wheels
Bringing the farm to life.

It's never a job,
But a family tradition.
Never a question,
But a gut intuition.

Plant, grow,
Tend, harvest.
A connection to nature
In the strongest amongst us.

Passion driven,
Pride in our land,
Hard work in our blood,
Strength and knowledge in our hands.

Next / Graduate

The places you've been
Are stones on the road.
Leading you to the places
You never knew you'd want to go.

The road wasn't straight,
Nor will it ever be.
Keep your head up,
Yet stay grounded as a tree.

For what was once easy,
Will certainly become hard.
And what was once familiar,
Will feel distant from that old backyard.

With faith by your side
And curiosity in your head.
You will push through any doubts
And be true to you instead.

Experiences teach us
That is in our nature to grow.
Hold on to your dreams,
And welcome the next chapter of the you show.

Grown

My heart walked
Out the door today.
It chose a path,
And went on it's way.

Jumped from my chest,
Ran towards a star.
Chasing life,
Unknown yet how far.

Possibilities endless,
Yet my soul craves that beat,
My heart once gave me,
Before it sprouted two feet.

Heartbeat to man,
Child to friend.
Connected for always,
Bonds strong to the end.

Aging

Toss and turn
Aches, burns
Oh, to have my body.

My eyes deceiving
My soul unaware
Oh, to have my mind.

Energy around me
Spirits lifted
Oh, to have my youth.

Adventures gained
Treasures discovered
Oh, to have my wisdom.

Gates of gold
Pathways of purity
Oh, to feel no pain.

Rejoined together
At last, I embrace
My body welds with my mind.

Resting

It's time.
The days behind me,
Feeling a two directional pull.
But still unsure..

I'm ready.
I've given and received,
Persevering in times of dark.
But still unsure..

I'm scared.
Memories, moments,
What will come of them?
Still so unsure..

They know.
I see my love,
It walks the earth still.
Now, I rest.

www.ingramcontent.com/pod-product-compliance
Lightning Source LLC
LaVergne TN
LVHW050249200726
843509LV00015B/2952